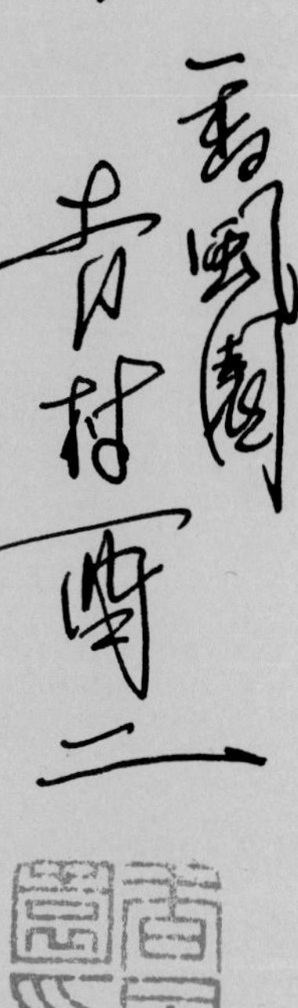

Yoshimura School of Bonsai

COMMEMORATIVE ALBUM

Marking 25 Years of Bonsai Instruction

The Muriel R. Leeds Collection

By
Yuji Yoshimura

This is number 219 from a limited edition of 500 copies

Yoshimura School of Bonsai

COMMEMORATIVE ALBUM

Marking 25 Years of Bonsai Instruction

The Muriel R. Leeds Collection

By
Yuji Yoshimura

Editor
Edwin C. Symmes, Jr.

Assistant Editors
Edward M. Watzik
Dorothy O'Quinn

Photography
Yuji Yoshimura
Muriel R. Leeds

Cover photo
The story of this magnificent Satsuki azalea begins on page 38.

Photo opposite
The full story about this Japanese spindle tree or Winged euonymus can be found on page 45.

Published by
Yoshimura School of Bonsai
P.O. Box 265 Scarborough Station
Briarcliff Manor, N.Y. 10510

Book Design by Edwin C. Symmes, Jr.

Manufactured in the United States of America

ISBN 0-916352-08-0 Paperback
ISBN 0-916352-09-9 Library Binding

LCC No. applied for.

Distributed by
Symmes Systems
Box 8101, Atlanta, Georgia 30306

The bonsai garden faces south for maximum exposure to the sun.
The benches contain an automatic watering system.
Details begin on page 60.

1976

A note from the Editor

A warm smile lit Mr. Yoshimura's face when he answered, "This will be the first book in the history of bonsai to show year by year changes of individual bonsai for over 10 years."

We were just beginning to talk about the **COMMEMORATIVE ALBUM.** To my knowledge, there has been no book devoted to this topic in English or Japanese, and Yuji's answer had just confirmed that this would be a unique publication in bonsai literature.

An exciting idea, I thought, but what a long project. We need to start photographing the trees immediately in order to have a series of photos over the next 10 years. And, where would we find this group of 50 bonsai Yuji was thinking of showing?

As I voiced my comments about the problems of time and subject matter, Yuji smiled again. "We already have the photographs of my student's bonsai as they were 10 years ago. Now we need only to photograph the collection as it is today and write the text."

A publication of this magnitude is a result of a major effort by many people. First, came Yuji's vision to begin the photography when the trees were newly found materials. Next, the dedication of Muriel R. Leeds, who has followed Mr. Yoshimura's instruction in the classical techniques of bonsai culture for over a decade. Her daily care has kept the collection healthy and on course in its development. Several other people have made extensive contributions, including Edward M. Watzik in New York and Dorothy O'Quinn in Georgia whose editorial comments have molded the book. Additional assistance has been provided by Raymond A. Schieber and Ethel H. Strain.

I am especially pleased to have had a part in this very exciting book because it also marks the 25th anniversary of bonsai instruction by Mr. Yoshimura. I hasten to point out that this is not 25 years of involvement in bonsai, but a quarter century of classical bonsai instruction.

Mr. Yoshimura's early training came from working at his father's bonsai garden in Japan. Then came professional bonsai education and more work before he began giving formal lessons. His dedication to classical bonsai art has been lifelong. It seems particularly fitting to mark a quarter century of personal bonsai instruction with the publication of this precedent setting book.

Edwin C. Symmes, Jr.

TABLE OF CONTENTS

1976

MUGO PINE, *Pinus mugo.*
Style: Cascade.
Size: Height 11 in., width 26 in.
Container: Red glazed irregular round, diameter 16 in., depth 5-1/2 in.

This tree was a fifteen year old seedling when it was purchased from nursery stock in Westchester County, New York. It was created into a bonsai in 1960. After ten years of training, the growth of the back of the tree had become more interesting than the front. The back was then chosen as the viewing side. To create a more refined design, a twig from the parent tree was used as a scion to graft a branch onto the back of the tree. This was done in February of 1971. The unusual container was made in the spring of 1976 by Joseph Godwin in Tarrytown, New York. It was designed by the author and made under his guidance. Although it is a new container, the shape, color and glaze are such that it appears to be very old.

1966

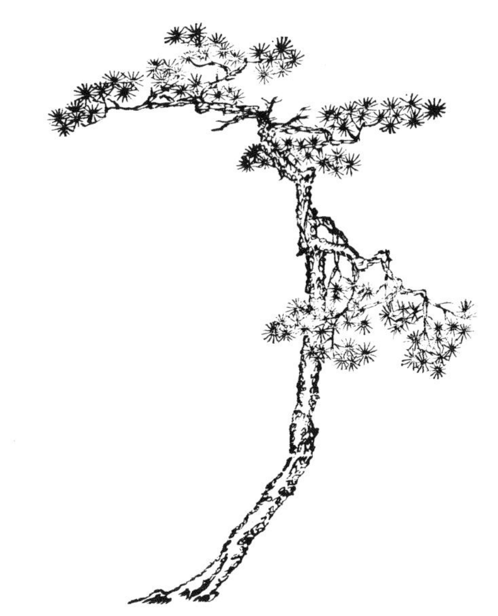

1. EVERGREENS

CULTURE OF PINES

Pines, *Pinus* are revered as one of the finest materials from which to create bonsai. They are easily obtained, either from nursery stock or from areas where they grow naturally. Pines are a "must" in the collection of any bonsai lover.

Pines are superior for conversion to bonsai for many reasons. Once they have been established in the container they are almost immune to dehydration. They are quite resistent to insects and diseases and do not need repotting very often. Most pines require full sun, except during the winter. Aesthetically, the rough bark gives the tree an aged appearance. Altering the shape is easy because of the flexibility of the trunk and branches.

The timing for transplanting is more critical than that of other evergreen needle species such as juniper, cypress and cryptomeria. The best time is just before new shoots start to grow. Repotting should be avoided when needles are new and still soft. If a white fungus-like substance (mycorrhiza) is found in the soil or root system, do not remove it. This fungus is beneficial to the pine and should be transferred with the plant when repotting.

Most pines do not produce new shoots from old wood. Some exceptions to this are the pitch pine, *P. rigida* and pinyon pine, *P. cembroides.*

Some unusual varieties of pine, such as dwarf eastern white pine, *P. strobus "nana,"* dragon's eye pine, *P. densiflora "oculis draconis,"* and Japanese five-needle pine, *P. parviflora,* are often grafted. It is necessary to select grafted material very carefully. The graft should be as low as possible to the roots. If the graft is too high it will detract from the bonsai even though the shape of the trunk and the branch pattern are excellent.

Succeeding needles will gradually decrease in size after the tree has been growing in a small container for awhile. Pines grow very slowly, but with proper care you will enjoy their beauty for a lifetime.

For indoor culture, Norfolk Island pine, *Araucaria heterophylla; exselsa,* is most suitable. The Norfolk Island pine can be grown from seed, cuttings or layering. The trunk and branches can be cut back drastically. This will encourage a thicker trunk and fuller foliage.

CULTURE OF BLACK PINES and MUGO PINES

There are over ten species of two and three needle pines which are excellent for creating bonsai. The Japanese black pine, *P. thunbergii* and mugo pine, *P. mugo* are favorites of bonsai lovers.

A sandy soil mixture is the most suitable for potting. During the training period, water often and feed well, this will encourage their health and needle length. Do not concentrate on the development of short, compact needles until the trunk and branches have reached a satisfactory stage of development.

The timing for maintenance trimming of pines is critical. As the new shoots appear, break two-thirds of the candle off with fingers or tweezers. This will be an on-going process as all of the buds do not appear at the same time.

Needle length can be decreased by cutting back the current and previous year's growth at the end of the growing season (late summer to early fall in the Northeast United States). To do this, use sharp scissors; insert the point above the cluster of needles and cut the twig at an angle (not across the twig), leaving five clustered needles. Do not cut the needles as this will cause them to turn an unsightly brown. New buds will develop at the point of the cut or between needles. Twig development can be increased by applying this same technique, but only at the beginning of the growing season (spring to early summer in the Northeast United States).

Pines often also have a short growth period in the fall which produces a swelling of the branches. Since wires used to shape the tree will not expand with this growth, the bark may be damaged by wire cut, therefore they should be removed before growth periods.

Pay particular attention to watering in autumn. Due to the sandy soil and the dryness of this season, pines require watering more frequently than other species, such as deciduous trees.

MUGO PINE, *Pinus mugo.*
Style: Semi-cascade.
Size: Height 13 in., width 25 in., depth 23 in.
Container: Brown unglazed square, 10 x 10 x 5 in.

The author obtained this material from a nursery in Westchester County in the spring of 1959. Jane Scott, who was attending the author's weekend classes at Juanita Schiff's residence in Ossining, New York, spent two days converting it into a bonsai. For this reason it was named "Jane's Pine." In 1960 the tree was displayed at an outdoor exhibition of the Cleveland Art Museum, where the author was lecturing. To maintain its beauty, the fine branches have been wired and the new growth trimmed back at least once a year. The 1972 photograph shows the tree before the work was completed. By 1976 the creation of this bonsai had almost reached its goal. In the future the tree may be cut back and the twigs above the middle branches thinned out.

1966

1972

1976

MUGO PINE, *Pinus mugo.*
Style: Slanting.
Height: 15 in.
Container: Brown unglazed rectangular
15 x 10-1/4 x 5 in.

When this bonsai was created in 1959, it was 18 inches tall and planted in a rectangular redwood box 25 x 19-1/2 x 4-1/2 inches. Because the author was living on Spring Valley Road in Ossining, N.Y. at the time, the bonsai was named "Spring Valley." Originally the tree was planted as a root-over-rock style as shown in the 1966 photograph. The tree was redesigned in 1972. It was changed to a slanting style and planted in a container without the rock. The design was improved in 1976, as shown in the photo above right, when a thick surface root, which was spoiling the overall effect, was removed from the left side.

1976

1966

MUGO PINE, *Pinus mugo.*
Style:
A. Three tree group planting.
B. Two tree group planting.
Height:
A. 5 in.
B. 9 in.
Container:
A. Brown unglazed irregular oval, flat clay, 18 x 12 x 1 in.
B. Brown unglazed rectangular, 22 x 9 x 2-1/2 in.

In 1965 Mugo pine seedlings, about three years old, were planted on a rock found in northern New York State. Before the trees were planted, No. 20 copper wire was attached to the rock with cement in six places as the 1964 photograph shows. The trees grew out of proportion, and in 1972 they were removed from the rock and two separate group plantings were created, as shown in photographs A and B. Photograph A-2 shows the three-tree group three years later.

B 1976

1964

1966

B. 1966

A. 1972

A 2. 1976

NISHIKI BLACK PINE, *Pinus thunbergii* var. *corticosa.*

Style: Informal upright.

Height: 19 in.

Container: Dark gray unglazed rectangular, 18 x 14 x 4 in.

A scion of cork bark pine was grafted onto the understock of a Japanese black pine, *Pinus thunbergii* in 1964. During the next twelve years the tree grew from a small grafted bud to a height of 19 inches. The bark is now well corked and the bottom of the trunk is four inches in diameter. An additional seven inches of height will improve the appearance of this tree. Three more years of growth should produce the desired height. During this time the thickness of the trunk will also increase to approximately double in diameter and the first stage of its creation will be complete. This bonsai will then have great dignity and beauty.

1966

1970

1976

1976

JAPANESE BLACK PINE,
Pinus thunbergii.
Style: Informal upright.
Height: 23 in.
Container: Brown unglazed rectangular, 15 x 9-1/2 x 5 in.

This tree was obtained as a bonsai in 1964 from a nursery near Los Angeles, California. Originally it was grown from seed and trained by a Japanese-American for about 15 years. The direction of the viewing side was changed and many roots and undesirable branches were removed. At the present time the bark is not rough enough and the needles are too long. It will be drastically pruned in 1978, and planted in a larger container. An improved bonsai should result.

1966

PITCH PINE, *Pinus rigida.*
Style: Cascade driftwood.
Height: 23 in.
Container: Red glazed irregular round 17 x 5 in.

A naturally contorted pitch pine was collected in the mountainous region of northern New York State in 1967. The tree was planted in the ground to improve its survival chances. In the spring of 1968 it was transplanted into a redwood box. The first three photographs show the tree in its original form. Because it was necessary to remove so many roots when it was dug from the rocky ground, the main trunk gradually became weak, and in 1968 it died. Fortunately, many suckers grew from the bottom, as the 1969 photograph shows. In the spring of 1971, four years after it was collected, the tree was planted in a container about 18 inches long and four inches deep and the shaping of the suckers was begun. The dead main trunk was cut short with an electric saw and wood carving tools were used to create the driftwood. The 1976 photograph shows the newly trained suckers had grown enough to justify transplanting into a bonsai container.

1968

1968

1968

1969

1976

CULTURE OF CRYPTOMERIAS

Cryptomeria, *C. japonica* prefer moist air and require watering more frequently than pines and spruce.

While several varieties are interesting, the common cryptomeria is the best choice for bonsai because of its fine twigs and short, compact needle growth. Its natural growth habit is a very straight trunk and should be grown only in the formal upright style.

Cryptomeria produces new shoots throughout the growing season which permits development of a compact shape in a relatively short period of time. This makes it necessary to be alert to new growth and pinch back accordingly.

Transplanting presents no unusual problems, but should not be done if there is a possibility that the night temperature will drop below 40° F. Of all the conifers, cryptomeria is the easiest to grow from cuttings or by layering.

1972

CRYPTOMERIA, *Cryptomeria japonica.*
Style: Formal upright.
Height: 27 in.
Container: Brown half glazed oval,
22 x 17 x 2-1/2 in.

This bonsai was started in 1964 from three year old material grown from a cutting. As the projected finished height is to be about 37 inches, a strong new shoot is always kept as a terminal each time the branches are thinned and cut back, as shown in the 1972 photograph. The 1976 photograph shows the terminal without long shoots to give an impression of the way it will look when the tree has matured.

1976

CULTURE OF JUNIPERS

Junipers, *Juniperus* are one of the easiest species to develop into bonsai and are highly recommended for the novice. There is a large variety of junipers suitable for bonsai culture, including fantastically beautiful material that grows abundantly in most areas of the United States and can be collected in the wild. Junipers adapt more readily to transplanting than most of the other evergreen needle species because they have an abundance of fine feeder roots. Repot and shape at any time of the year except during the dormant period. As with cypress and cryptomeria, the branches can be bent and wired easily to create desirable shapes, but be careful not to exert too much pressure or the branch will split at the joint.

General care of junipers is similar to that described for cypress, but red spiders can be a problem, particularly in the dry season if the tree is in a shady spot with little air circulation.

1976

CHINESE JUNIPER,
Juniperus chinensis.
Style: Informal upright driftwood.
Height: 23 in.
Container: White crackle glazed,
17 x 11-1/2 x 3-1/2 in.

This material was obtained from a northern California nursery. In 1967 it was created into a slanting style bonsai. The unusual design of this tree combines a straight trunk in the lower one-third with a curved upper part. While this design does not follow the usual guidelines of classical bonsai style, the driftwood, which was created in 1970, has an interesting shape and enhances the design of the tree. A further refinement can be accomplished by planting it in an oval container of the same size and color as the present rectangular one.

SARGENT JUNIPER, *Juniperus chinensis* var. *sargentii.*
Style: Informal upright twin-trunk.
Height: 15 in.
Container: Red unglazed rectangular, 13-1/2 x 9-1/2 x 4-1/4 in.

This cutting was made by the author in 1939 in Japan where it grew until it was imported to the United States in 1960. A large container was used to encourage growth and thus develop a heavier trunk.

This tree has a basic weakness. The fi branch on the left side of the main tru has grown vigorously upward. Cons quently, each year this branch will ha to be wired and gradually brought dow Also, the twigs will be trimmed twice year to develop density and hide t joint of the branch at the trunk. T 1976 photograph was taken befc trimming.

1966

1969

19

19

1976

AMARIX SAVIN JUNIPER, *Juniperus sabina* cult. *tamariscifolia.*

·yle: Informal upright multiple trunk.

eight: 14 in.

ɔntainer: Brown unglazed rectangular, 18-1/2 x 12 x 3 in.

·ter nine years of cultivation, the appearance of this juniper with its fine ›edles resembles part of a deep natal forest. The original nursery stock as transferred to a five gallon training ›n in 1964. Bonsai training began in)67. The 1969 photograph was taken ter the removal of several branches. emoval of the thick side branch in)72 left a thin main trunk. This trunk ll be developed in the future and the ›nsai will be planted on a flat rock. ıe anticipation of future changes is ıe of the finest pleasures in the creaɔn of bonsai art.

1969

PFIZER JUNIPER, *Juniperus chinensis* cult. *pfizeriana.*
Style: Cascade.
Size: Top to bottom, 36 in.
Container: Dark brown unglazed hexagonal, diameter 10 in. depth 8 in.

The cascade style of this tree was created in 1967 from northern California nursery stock. The desired trunk length was reached in 1975 and it was planted into a new container. When the branches become more dense and the base of the trunk thickens, this bonsai will be a fine example of the formal cascade style.

1967

1976

CULTURE OF FIVE-NEEDLE PINES

The following five-needle pines may all be considered for bonsai development: Japanese five-needle pine, *P. parviflora* is highly desirable for bonsai because of its short needles and thin twigs; limber pine, *P. flexilis,* western white pine, *P. monticola* and bristlecone pine, *P. aristata* have short needles, similar to the Japanese five-needle pine, but the twigs are heavier. Bristlecone pines tend to develop white resin spots which detract from their appearance. Eastern white pine, *P. strobus* has long, thin needles—the variety *"Nana"* is considered best for bonsai. Exercise care in selecting the *"Nana"* variety; it is usually grafted and if the graft has not been made carefully it will show as the tree matures and mar the appearance of the bonsai.

The recommended technique used to develop short needles on the five-needle pine is to pull out all of the new needles every two years before the needles harden. Pull out only the needles—leave the sheath. The new, shorter needles may not appear until the following year.

JAPANESE FIVE-NEEDLE PINES,
Pinus parviflora.

Style:
1. Slanting.
2. Slanting.
3. Informal upright.

Height:
1. 4 in.
2. 10 in.
3. 6 in.

Container:
1. Brown unglazed round, 6-1/2 x 2 in.
2. Red unglazed rectangular, 10 x 7-1/2 x 3 in.
3. Red unglazed rectangular, 5-1/2 x 4-1/2 x 2 in.

These pines were grafted on black pine stock in 1961. In 1962 they were planted on a rock, as shown in the 1964 photograph. As the trees grew the trunks became heavy and harmony between the trees and the rock was lost. The trees were removed from the rock and created into the individual small bonsai shown in the 1976 photograph.

1964

1976

WESTERN FIVE-NEEDLE PINE,
Pinus monticola.
Style: Informal upright.
Height: 25 in.
Container: Brown unglazed rectangular, 13-1/2 x 12-1/2 x 4-1/2 in.

This tree was collected in the Midwest. It was purchased by the author at an east coast nursery in 1961. At that time the estimated age was 25 years. The tree was kept in the ground for two years. All unwanted branches were removed and new shoots were pruned regularly. In 1963 the roots were pruned and the tree was planted in the container shown in the 1966 photograph. A weakness of this tree was the abrupt decrease in the diameter of the trunk. To thicken the upper part of the trunk a long new shoot was encouraged to grow, as shown in the 1971 photograph.

In 1972-73 the trunk of the tree, from bottom to terminal, was tied to a one inch stainless steel pipe to correct the direction of the main line. All the main branches needed to be pulled down. This was accomplished by attaching No. 18 copper wire to each main branch, pulling the branch down to the desired position, and anchoring the wire to another strong wire which was fastened lengthwise around the container. These corrections were completed within one year.

1966

1974

1971

1976

CULTURE OF DWARF BOX

Buxus microphylla var. *compacta,* also called Kingsville box, is a treasure to add to any bonsai collection. It grows well in shade, and can be transplanted at any time during the growing season. New buds grow from old branches, even when drastically pruned, and scars heal very quickly.

Dwarf box can be grown easily from cuttings. It has one weak point—the branches are brittle and extreme care must be taken when bending to shape or they will snap.

KINGSVILLE DWARF BOX, *Buxus microphylla* var. *compacta.*
Style: Informal upright.
Height: 4 in.
Container: Brown unglazed rectangular, 3-1/2 x 2-1/2 x 1-1/2 in.
This tree was started from a cutting in 1960. It has been growing in the present container since 1964.

1976

CULTURE OF CYPRESS

The name "cypress" is commonly applied to three different genera: *Cupressus* (True cypress), *Chamaecyparis* (False cypress) and *Taxodium* (Bald cypress, a deciduous tree). *Chamaecyparis* is the most popular genus for bonsai.

The hinoki cypress, *C. obtusa* and sawara cypress, *C. pisifera* are favorites among bonsai lovers. The needles are compact, the branches are flexible and can be shaped very easily with wire. Care must be used to avoid splitting at the joints of the branches. Like the juniper, they are excellent material for the beginner to work with.

During the growing season cypress prefer a sunny spot. They will grow in shade but will not remain compact. The foliage should be thinned out twice a year.

Transplanting is relatively easy and it is safe to do at any time except during the dormant period. Cypress propagate easily from cuttings.

DWARF HINOKI CYPRESS, *Chamaecyparis obtusa* "Nana."
Style: Root-over-rock.
Height: 18 in.
Container: Brown unglazed shallow oval, 21 x 13-1/2 x 2 in.
This tree was originally created from nursery stock and planted directly over carved feather rock in 1964. A container three inches deep was used to develop a thicker trunk and more growth on the branches. In 1976, after it had attained the correct trunk size and density of branches, it was planted in the present container. This container is ideal in color and shape to complement the beauty of this bonsai.

1976

CULTURE OF SPRUCES

There are many kinds of spruce, *Picea.* The following species are suitable material for the advanced student of bonsai: Norway spruce, *P. abies,* Colorado spruce, *P. pungens* and Alberta spruce, *P. glauca.* These species are noteworthy for their adaptability to shallow containers and for growing on a rock. Alterations to shape is relatively easy as the branches do not break or split easily.

Maintenance trimming is done once or twice a year. New growth should be pinched back before the needles are fully developed. If upper branches are allowed to overgrow without thinning, the inside branches will die.

The majority of common spruce are usually grown from seeds or cuttings. Some unusual varieties are grafted. For aesthetic appeal, select trees with many large surface roots.

Spruce do not require frequent repotting. Most of the fine feeder roots of the spruce are at the ends of the heavy roots. This must be considered when root pruning, as drastic pruning or cutting them too short may remove too many feeder roots and will cause the tree to die.

Spruce require full sun and will not grow in shade. Spider mites can be a problem, but otherwise the spruce is relatively disease and pest resistent.

ALBERTA SPRUCE,
Picea glauca var. *conica.*
Style: Formal upright twin-trunk.
Height: 42 in.
Container: Brown half glazed oval, 30x 23 x 3 in.

1966

This tree was growing in the ground in a nursery in Westchester County when it was acquired by the author in 1960. It was cut back to one third of its original height and all unnecessary branches were removed to complete the over-all design. The direction of the main branches was changed by using heavy wire (No. 8 to No. 14). This correction did not change the basic shape of the bonsai because the development had been retarded by removing many roots and branches. By 1968 the tree had recovered sufficiently from the initial shock of severe pruning for the wiring of the fine branches to begin. All wiring has continued almost every year since that time. In 1974 the tree was transplanted into a larger container of identical shape which harmonizes so well with this particular bonsai. As the 1976 photographs shows, the main branches have become powerful after 16 years of training. In a few years, when the lower branches become stronger, the first stage of creation will be completed.

1976

2. DECIDUOUS

CULTURE OF ELMS

The common English name "elm" is used for the genus *Ulmus* of the family *Ulmaceae.* The zelkova, which also belongs to this family, is often confused with the elms because they are so similar. The elm has softer wood and rougher bark and can usually be identified by these characteristics.

Chinese elm, *Ulmus parvifolia,* became popular in the United States as bonsai material because of its resistance to Dutch Elm disease, but many other elms are suitable for bonsai culture. Because elms easily produce new buds on branches which develop into fine twigs with small leaves, they are adaptable to many styles.

Elms can easily be propagated by layering or cuttings and are very suitable for miniature bonsai. Except for cultivars which grow in the southern United States, they are winter hardy.

CHINESE ELM, *Ulmus parvifolia.*
Style: Informal upright twin-trunk.
Height: 22 in.
Container: Dark blue glazed round,
10 x 5 in.
This tree was estimated to be approximately 40 years old in 1960 when it was imported from Japan. The photograph taken in 1966 shows its original design. The round moon-shaped branch at the bottom of the main trunk was bent, and an inarch graft was applied to the bottom right side of the trunk. This design is referred to in Japan as the "flower basket elm" or "full moon elm." The rounded trunk gradually decayed in 1970. Two points are noteworthy in the refined version: A terminal was clearly created on the main trunk, and the two trunks were pulled together as shown in the 1976 photograph. In the future it is hoped to create a new branch on the left side where the main trunk curves to the right. This will further improve the shape of this bonsai.

1966

1970

1976

CULTURE OF ZELKOVAS

Zelkova is a genus of the elm family. There are a few mutations such as dwarf types, rough bark and variegated leaves.

This is one of the most suitable species for bonsai culture because of its hard wood, small leaves and tolerance of dehydration. Due to its natural growth habit, the broom style is best for bonsai. It is also one of the best species to use when creating a group planting.

Zelkova can be propagated by layering or cuttings. It is winter hardy and easily transplanted.

1976

ZELKOVA, *Zelkova serrata.*
Style: Broom.
Height: 15 in.
Container: Brown unglazed oval
15 x 10 x 3 in.
This bonsai was imported from Japan as a seedling in 1960. The estimated age is approximately 28 years.

CULTURE OF MAPLES

There are over 100 species in the maple family and several hundred cultivars. In Asia, maples have been used in pots or as ornamental trees in the garden for over 300 years. There are many variations in the shape of leaves, color and growth habits.

Acer palmatum and its varieties are especially popular for bonsai culture. In comparison to other species it is safe to transplant once the buds start to grow and before the leaves are fully opened. Because they develop many feeder roots, the trees retain their vigor and the buds do not break off easily.

Large branches can be removed and the trunk cut back severely with assurance that the tree will live and new buds will develop. It is important to use tree paint on all large scars for proper healing. With drastic pruning, a bonsai can be created from an overgrown tree purchased from a nursery, or an ordinary tree growing in the garden. This should be done in the early spring just when new buds start to swell.

The trident maple, *Acer buergerianum* is ideal for rock planting because the roots will attach themselves firmly to the rock. When shaping by wire, care must be taken to avoid breaking the branches as even the tender new shoots are very brittle. Since the fast growing new shoots have soft bark, they should be carefully watched for the first sign of swelling so the wire can be removed before damage occurs. During the growing season, damage can result within a few weeks. The foliage of this species is broader and thinner than other species. In order to prevent the tips of the leaves from turning brown, the tree must not be allowed to dehydrate.

Defoliation should be done only on healthy trees and not after the growing season. It should never be done on less vigorous varieties such as *Acer palmatum dissectum.*

Growth is easily encouraged by planting in a deep pot with coarse soil for good drainage. Technically it is difficult to create fine delicate twigs without weakening the plant. Maples are winter-hardy but all wires on the branches should be removed before the arrival of cold weather.

JAPANESE COMMON MAPLE,
Acer palmatum.
Style: Nine tree group planting.
Height: 23 in.
Container: Brown unglazed oval straight-sided 20 x 15 x 1 in.

In 1964 this group was created with three to five year old seedlings. Within seven years the original container became too small to keep the trees in good health. As a result this bonsai group became dehydrated. It was then planted in a wooden flat, 17 x 14 x 3 inches for two years (1974-76). After it recovered, the group was planted in the present container.

1964

1976

JAPANESE COMMON MAPLE, *Acer palmatum.*
Style: Informal upright.
Height: 28 in.
Container: Brown unglazed round 9 x 9 in.

This tree was grown in a nursery in Long Island, New York and created into a bonsai in 1964. In 1976 the estimated age was 27 years; the surface roots were well established and the trunk was well developed. Having been in the same container for twelve years, it is now time to transplant it into a larger container.

1966

1976

TRIDENT MAPLE, *Acer buergerianum.*
Style: Informal upright twin-trunk.
Height: 24 in.
Container: Gray glazed rectangular 16 x 11-1/2 x 4-1/2 in.

This tree was dug from the ground and planted in a deep wooden container in 1968. The first photograph was taken after it was reduced from a height of six feet to about one and one half feet. In the 1972 photograph, unnecessary new shoots have been eliminated and the wiring and repotting continued. In 1973, when the new leaves started opening, they suddenly wilted. A fungus had attacked the terminal where a one inch scar from the drastic cut remained, even though the scar had been well treated with tree paint at the time. To stop the fungus, Benomyl was used three times. Spagnum moss was wrapped on the branches where the leaves had wilted to keep them moist until they recovered. The disaster was over within three months. The 1973 photograph shows the tree without pruning. This was done

1968

1972

1973

1976

in order to create longer and heavier branches, which the photograph also shows. The next year the branches were pruned back, keeping only two or three buds. They were then allowed to grow again. In 1976 the tree was transplanted to a fine bonsai container. Large scars still remain on the trunk in many places but if it is kept under ideal conditions, the scars should disappear within three years. It will probably take another five years to become a twin-trunk style bonsai rather than just a stick with a root.

JAPANESE CUT-LEAF RED MAPLE,
Acer palmatum var. *dissectum.*
Style: Informal upright.
Height: 42 in.
Container: Redwood tub 18 x 18 x 17 in.
The original tree was imported from Japan about 1930. (It is not known whether it was a bonsai at that time.) It was planted in open ground on the property of Detmer's Nursery in Tarrytown, New York where it remained until 1964. It was then designed as a bonsai and planted in a green glazed round container of Kuang-tung ware, 14-1/2 inches across and 11 inches deep. It was repotted each year and its beauty continued to improve. In April 1976 it was blown over during a heavy windstorm and its most important branch, the lowest branch on the right side, was broken. Only one foot of the branch remained. On May 24th, even though the season for repotting *dissectums* had passed, it was decided to transplant the tree into a wooden tub. Hopefully this would produce new growth on the damaged branch. The bonsai will be kept in this tub until the spring of 1978 when it will be transplanted into a new container. An ideal container for this bonsai is a glazed greenish-beige irregular round, 20 inches in diameter and eight to ten inches deep.

1966

1976

CULTURE OF WILLOWS

Willow, *Salicaceae*, is a fast growing softwood plant of 350 known species. It is easily propagated by cuttings or layering. Cuttings of one to two inches in diameter will root and grow if carefully attended. Willows like wet ground; an adequate supply of water is necessary for the branches to become long and graceful as shown in the photograph. From late spring to early autumn it is advisable to keep the potted plant in a basin of water to prevent drying.

Following their natural habit of growth, willow bonsai can be created into slanting, semi-cascade or cascade styles. The container selected must allow the long branches to hang down. Willows are winter hardy, and one of the best cultivars is "ROKKAUDO," shown on page 35.

There are two important considerations when potting willows:

1. The size of the container should be larger and deeper than normally used for bonsai because of the tree's demand for water.
2. The most suitable color for a willow container is a whitish glaze. The soft green foliage will show up best against the white glaze, providing a cool appearance in summer.

Willows should be cut back drastically when repotting. Both potting and drastic pruning are usually done in the spring and again at the beginning of summer. New shoots of less than one foot should be trained downward with copper wire. Since willows grow quickly, the shoots must be carefully watched to prevent damage to the bark. When the new shoots become longer than one foot they can be trained by hand. Start bending the shoots several times a day in the desired direction. After about a week of training, you will find the branches retaining the shape you desire.

Aphids and caterpillars are common pests of willow and must be destroyed before they attack the foliage. Tree paint should be used on any pruning thicker than a pencil, for once the trunk is attacked by pests it will decay.

BABYLON WEEPING WILLOW,
Salix babylonica.
Style: Slanting.
Height: 34 in.
Container: White crackle-glazed round 18 x 9 in.

When this bonsai was imported from Japan in 1960 it was about two feet high and the trunk was two fingers thick. As the tree grew it was moved into a larger container. The container shown in the photographs has been used since 1964. The 1966 photographs show the tree soon after being trimmed and one month later. This bonsai is kept in a corner of a porch, where it gives great joy to its owner.

June 1966

August 1966

1976

CULTURE OF GINKGOS

The Ginkgo belongs to one of eight families of *Coniferae.* It is winter hardy and has vigorous growth when planted in a pot with good drainage and fed with high nitrogen fertilizer.

Buds are produced on heavy branches or on the trunk, but not as abundantly as with the maple or zelkova. Since ginkgo wood is not very hard, it is always wise to use tree paint to cover pruning scars. Check paint periodically for wear.

Ginkgos are easily grown from cuttings. This species is not suitable for group planting as the large leaves cannot be reduced in size. Neither are they easily adaptable to rock planting because the roots will not attach themselves to the rock.

1968

1969

GINKGO, *Ginkgo biloba.*
Style: Informal upright.
Height: 40 in.
Container: Brown unglazed rectangular
16-1/2 x 12 x 5 in.

This bonsai was originally grown in the ground at Elizabeth N. Humes' "Bonsai Material Garden." In the spring of 1968 she shared her excellent bonsai material with fellow students. The trees grown in her garden were trident maple, such as the one shown on page 33, flowering quince, cherry, larch, ginkgo and others. This tree was dug with bare roots and planted in a deep container as shown in the 1968 photograph. The original height of the tree was about six feet. When it was dug, the back half was cut away and the height was reduced to three feet. The following year it produced many new shoots on the trunk, and after eight years it began to show the true beauty of its shape. At least another five years will be necessary to heal the scars where the heavy branches were removed, and to develop denser foliage.

1976

1976

CULTURE OF HORNBEAMS and BIRCHES

The hornbeam, *Carpinus* and birch, *Betula* are popular trees for bonsai. Either the American or Asiatic variety is suitable for informal, upright, slanting or group planting styles.

Both trees have large thin leaves which require special attention to prevent burning by strong sun and dehydration. Defoliation is not recommended because it causes the fine twigs to die. Care must be taken to keep strong new shoots from growing near the bottom of the trunk or at the terminal as they take nourishment away from other parts of the tree and cause a weak uneven growth.

RED-LEAFED HORNBEAM,
Carpinus laxiflora.
Style: Informal twin-trunk.
Height: 24 in.
Container: Reddish unglazed oval
19 x 12 x 3 in.

This conventional twin-trunk bonsai was imported from Japan in 1968. It was trained as bonsai from a natural seedling. The age is estimated at 30 to 40 years.

3. FLOWERING AND FRUIT BEARING

CULTURE OF AZALEAS

The Azalea, *Rhododendron* is excellent bonsai material for those who enjoy flowering plants. There is a large assortment of azaleas to choose from with a variety of flower colors and growth habits. It is best to select plants with small leaves. Among the favorites for bonsai are *R. indicum, R. lateritium,* and *R. impeditum.* Azaleas grow vigorously in containers and produce flowers more readily than other flowering species such as camellia and myrtle. Virtually any desired shape can easily be created as the azalea may be cut back to old wood without damage to the plant's growth. One of the drawbacks when shaping azaleas is the brittleness of the branches which causes them to break easily. To compensate for this, alter the shape as soon as the new shoots develop, using No. 24 or No. 22 wire. Bending is easier if the plant is not watered for a day. This will cause a slight wilting condition which makes the branches more pliable.

Trimming may be somewhat confusing to the elementary student because of the growth habit of the azalea. At the end of the flowering season many new shoots appear below the point where the flowers bloomed and from the trunk and branches. While this profusion of growth may be confusing, it provides multiple selections for further branch development. Observe the en-

(continued on page 40)

SATSUKI AZALEA "Osakazuki,"
Rhododendron lateritium cult. *Osakazuki.*
Style: Informal upright.
Height: 32 in.
Container: Brown unglazed rectangular 21 x 14 x 7-1/2 in.

This azalea bonsai has an exceptiona[l] history. The original tree was approximately 250 years old. This was determined by the width at the bottom of the trunk which was 15 inches as shown in the 1966 photograph. In 1969 the tree died and lay on the ground for some time, but it had been too fine a specimen to lose. After giving four years of thought on how it could be restored six cuttings were attached to the branches of the old tree. The roots of the cuttings were wrapped with peat covered with gauze bandage and tied firmly with string. The 1973 photograph shows the tree with the cuttings attached. For the first year the entire tree was watered three times a day. The roots from the cuttings grew over the trunk and into the trunk as well. You can see the new growth which is creating the restored shape in the 1975 photograph. In 1976 the overall shape was more refined than in 1966, but it will still take a few more years for the roots to grow over and into the trunk deep enough to reach the ground. The restoration will be completed when the density of the terminal foliage increase.

1966

1973

April 1976

May 1976

(culture of azaleas
continued from page 38)

tire plant and remove any new growth not essential to the intended design. The growth which is retained should be trimmed back to one or two leaves. This will eventually increase the density of the foliage.

It is important that maintenance trimming be done at the proper time of the year. The flower buds for the following year develop on new growth at the end of summer, therefore trimming must be done in the late spring after the flowers have bloomed. In the northeastern United States do not trim after September or the number of flowers will be greatly reduced the following year.

Remember the basic rule for creating a fine bonsai in a short time: encourage growth to thicken the trunk, multiply branches and foliage. Continuous trimming in the early stages of development will minimize development. Maintenance trimming rules do not apply when the objective is to develop growth.

Transplanting should be done in the late spring after the flowers have

SATSUKI AZALEA
"SHINYO-NO-TSUKI,"
Rhododendron lateritium cult. *shinyo-no-tsuki.*
Style: Informal upright.
Height: 12 in.
Container: White crackle-glazed rectangular 17 x 11-1/2 x 3-1/2 in.
This bonsai was imported from Japan in 1960 with an estimated age of 10 years. Its flowers are single, dark pink with white centers, and three inches in diameter.

bloomed. Before replanting, wash the soil off completely using strong water pressure; a hose is very effective for this. The soil should be a course mixture of peat moss and garden loam and must be acid, preferably pH 5. The roots require a moist condition and will not endure if allowed to dry out. Azaleas may be propagated from cuttings or by layering.

Fading color and dropping leaves indicate the presence of lace bugs. These insects adhere to the underside of the leaves and suck the juices from the plant. Check frequently for signs of these bugs and remove them immediately.

1966

TRAY LANDSCAPE.
Height: 6 in.
Container: Brown unglazed oval
18 x 13 x 1-1/2 in.
The material used in this landscape consists of the following:

1. SATSUKI AZALEA, *Rhododendron lateritium.* White single flowers with pink stripes. Some flowers are pure white and some are pure pink. One plant.
2. JUNIPER, *Juniperus procumbens* var. *nana.* Three plants.
3. ILEX, *Ilex crenata.* One plant.
4. DWARF SAWARA CYPRESS, *Chamaecyparis pisifera* cult. *tsukumo hiba.* Two plants.
5. GOLDEN FERN, *Selaginella caulescens.*
6. Two rocks.

1976

CULTURE OF CAMELLIAS

Common camellia, *Camellia japonica* and Sasanqua camellia, *C. sasanqua* are very colorful when in bloom and add a bright accent to a bonsai display. They will grow well in shade and can be grown indoors. This plant requires a humid atmosphere to survive. When grown indoors brown leaf edges and dropping buds are signs of dehydration.

The camellia is similar to the azalea in that denser foliage and buds can be induced by cutting back to old wood. Branches and young shoots are very brittle and extreme care must be taken not to break them when shaping the plant.

It is particularly sensitive to dry atmosphere and low temperatures. The first frost will damage the soft buds. The sasanqua camellia is hardier than the common camellia and can endure temperatures as low as 32° F.

The roots of the camellia grow very rapidly which makes it necessary to repot once a year in the spring after the outside temperature remains above 45° F. If there is a possibility the temperature will drop below 45° F. after repotting, the plant should be brought indoors. The roots of the camellia are very susceptible to damage, and will break easily if not handled with care. It is necessary to remove all of the old soil when repotting.

Wiring is done in the spring. The wired branches should be examined frequently as branch swelling during the growing season will cause the wire to scar the bark.

Follow the same method for maintenance trimming as that described for the azalea. Do not trim new growth during autumn or winter. Camellias can be propagated from cuttings, but it takes at least six months to establish a good root base for planting.

SASANQUA CAMELLIA,
Camellia sasanqua.
Pale pink single flower with white edge.
Style: Informal upright.
Height: 28 in.
Container: Dark blue glazed rectangular
16 x 11-1/2 x 3 in.

This tree was grown from a cutting. It was imported from Japan in 1960 at which time it was approximately 15 years old. Importation involved being transported with totally bare roots wrapped only with wet sphagnum moss. No additional water was given for one month. Upon arrival it was fumigated at 70 degrees for two hours. The 1966 photograph shows its vigorous growth after recovering from importation. In 1972 the tree was put in a large training pot to encourage a heavier trunk. It was transplanted into the present container in 1974.

1966

1976

1970

(sasanqua camellia description on page 44)

1976

SASANQUA CAMELLIA,
Camellia sasanqua.
White double flower.
Style: Cascade.
Height: 40 in.
Container: Yellow glazed hexagonal
9 in. across, 7-1/4 in. deep.

This tree was created into a cascade style in 1965. The plant used was ten years old, grown from a cutting. It was planted in a deep unglazed container for training purposes as the 1970 photograph shows. In 1974 the tree was transplanted into the present container. The line of the trunk and the proportion of the branches makes this a good example of the classical cascade style bonsai.

(photographs of this bonsai appear on page 43)

DWARF MYRTLE,
Myrtus communis microphylla.
Style: Informal upright, twin-trunk.
Height: 21 in.
Container: Brown unglazed rectangular
15-1/2 x 10-3/4 x 4 in.

Phyllis Wishnick, a fellow student, made a cutting of dwarf myrtle in 1969 and gave it to the present owner in 1972. (Students often exchange material with each other.) The photograph shows this bonsai after four years of training.

1976

CULTURE OF MYRTLES

Common myrtle or German myrtle, *Myrtus communis* has larger leaves than the dwarf myrtle, *M. communis* var. *microphylla,* but is very similar in appearance. White flowers develop on new growth in summer and produce black berries. Both common and dwarf myrtle have variegated varieties and are excellent plants for indoor bonsai, but can withstand temperatures of 35° F if the change is gradual.

It is fairly easy to create desirable shapes with these species as they can be cut back to old wood and will quickly develop new growth. Exercise care when shaping as the branches tend to split at the joint of the node. Myrtle is grown from cuttings.

Scale, aphids and mealy bugs are common to the myrtle. They attack the branches and leaves and should be removed immediately.

CULTURE OF EUONYMUS

Winged euonymus, *E. alatus* is winter hardy, reportedly to —30° F. It will withstand the winter in a cold frame or the pot can be buried in the ground. The Japanese clone, which is pictured in this album, has smaller leaves and thinner twigs than the variety common to the United States. The foliage of both varieties turns a bright red in autumn. Small clusters of berries hang from the branches enhancing the beauty of this plant. The pale yellow flowers are 1/8 inch in diameter and appear at the nodes.

Shaping technique is the same as for nishiki pine; the ornamental bark is similar in appearance, resembling cork. Do not wrap wire directly around the branches as this will chip the bark. Instead, protect the branch with padding, drape the wire over the pad, gently pull the branch to the desired position and anchor the wire to the container. The branches are brittle and will break easily.

Trimming should be done after buds are well developed. If these twigs are cut back before the buds are well established the plant will produce few flowers or berries. Cut back sucker growth immediately as it weakens the tree.

The euonymus grows easily from seed, cuttings, or layering. Transplanting and soil requirements are not unusual.

This deciduous tree is a treasure in a bonsai collection.

JAPANESE SPINDLE TREE:
WINGED EUONYMUS,
Euonymus alatus.
Style: Cascade.
Height: 21 in.
Container: Yellow glazed irregular round 11 x 11 x 6-1/2 in.

The bonsai was imported from Japan in 1960. It had been trained in containers for approximately 35 years. The two photographs made in 1966 show the viewing side and the reverse side. By 1969 the reverse side of the tree had gained character and was then chosen as the viewing side. After another seven years, it was transplanted into its present, ideal container. Over 50 years have now gone into the training of this bonsai and it has entered its final stage of creation (see color photo on page 2.)

1966

1966

1969

1976

4. PLANTING ON ROCKS

SARGENT JUNIPER, *Juniperus chinensis* var. *sargentii.*
Size: Height 14 in. including the rock, width 19 in.
Basin: White glazed rectangular 21-3/4 x 13-1/2 x 1-1/2 in.
Seven individual juniper cuttings, after five years' growth, were planted on this rock in 1972. These cuttings have been wired, pruned and fed each year. They are now developing nicely. The limestone rock with its marble stripes is in harmony with the fine green foliage of the Sargent junipers, creating a subtle beauty.

1976

JAPANESE BLACK PINE, *Pinus thunbergii.*
Height: 20 in.
Height of rock: 16 in.
Basin: Bronze oval 30 x 18-1/4 x 1-3/4 in.
This tree was 19 years old when it was planted on the rock in 1966. It was very delicate the first few years because the root ball had to be greatly reduced. In 1973 the rock was overturned during a powerful windstorm and the terminal of the tree was broken off. Although the tree survived, it had to be re-created.

1976

MUGO PINE, *Pinus mugo.*
Height: 14 in.
Basin: Brown unglazed outside, white glazed inside, oval 21 x 14 x 1-1/4 in.

In 1972 this tree was planted on a rock found in upper New York State. No. 18 wire was attached to the rock to hold the roots in place. Muck, a rich soil of peat and humus, was applied under and over the roots and then covered with moss. The rock proved unstable, so additional rocks were cemented to the bottom to make it stand upright. Each year the tree must be wired and pruned to maintain its beauty.

1976

TRIDENT MAPLE, *Acer buergerianum.*
Style: Multiple trunk.
Height: 18 in. including the rock.
Basin: Bronze oval 26 x 16 x 1-3/4 in.

Originally this rock had a sinuous style juniper with more than ten trunks planted on it. This was replaced in 1970 by the trident maple shown in the photograph. This maple was propagated by layering. Since it dries out faster than pines or junipers, it must be watered more frequently during the growing season. After four years of training, the maple is beginning to harmonize with the rock.

1976

BEAN FERN,
Drymoglossum microphyllum.
Size: Height 6 in., length 12 in., depth 8 in.
Basin: Bronze oval 26 x 16 x 1-3/4 in.

Bean fern belongs to the *Polypody* family with some 65 genera and about 1000 species growing abundantly in the tropics. Jane Scott, one of the first students to attend the Yoshimura School of Bonsai, and founder of the Umi Bonsai Society, brought this unusual plant back from Japan. This fern grows well on a rock and prefers a shady place with high humidity. In the winter it is kept with other rock plantings in a greenhouse where the temperature ranges from 45° F to 70° F. It has also survived in an outdoor cold frame where the temperature dropped below 30° F.

1976

DWARF ALBERTA SPRUCE,
Picea glauca conica.
Style: Five tree group planting.
Size: Height 19 in., including the rock, width 19 in.
Basin: Bronze oval 30 x 18-1/4 x 1-3/4 in.

1966

This is one of the earliest rock plantings made by the author after he arrived in New York from Japan. Cuttings of dwarf spruce were obtained from a nursery in Oregon and the rock was found in Northern New York State. From the time this rock planting was completed it has required special attention. It must be fed no more than is necessary to keep it healthy as it is difficult to restrict the growth of these trees (see 1966 and 1976 photographs). Even though the height has been controlled by pruning, the trees will probably have to be removed from the rock within five years as the trunks may become too thick.

1976

1976

BLAAUW JUNIPER,
Juniperus chinensis "Blaauw."
Style: Seven tree group planting.
Size: Height 14-1/2 in., length 28-1/2 in.
Basin: Bronze oval
30 x 18-1/4 x 1-3/4 in.

In 1967 eleven trees grown from cuttings for three years were made into a group planting on this rock. The photograph taken in 1968 shows the original shape. As the trees grew, the trunks and twigs thickened and in 1969 it was decided to eliminate four of the original group. As the 1976 photograph shows, a more sensitive beauty has been created.

1968

ARGENT JUNIPER, *Juniperus chinensis* var. *sargentii.*
tyle: Sinuous.
leight: 17 in.
asin: White glazed rectangular
21-3/4 x 13-1/2 x 1-1/2 in.

his five year old tree grown from a utting was planted on a rock in 1967. 1971, because the original rock was nstable, it was attached to a flat rock, nd several smaller rocks were added the bottom to make the base more ecure.

1976

BLACK BIRCH, *Betula fontinalis,* planted on a flat rock.
Style: Twin trunk.
Height: 18 in.
Basin: Bronze oval
30 x 18-1/4 x 1-3/4 in.

This natural seedling of black birch was found on a huge rock in Tarrytown, New York. Although naturally stunted material is often found on a rocky mountain, it is amazing that this tree had been growing for ten to fifteen years from a seed which had fallen into a crack. When collected in 1965 the tree was dug out easily. It had good compact roots, therefore it could be planted immediately on the flat granite rock. The height of

1965

the tree at that time was 16 inches. The transplanted tree is now eleven years old and the height and thickness of the trunk have not changed significantly. Its present health and beauty can be attributed to the use of bonsai culture techniques.

1976

JAPANESE FIVE-NEEDLE PINE, *Pinus parviflora* with JAPANESE AZALEA, *Rhododendron lateritum* "Hinode."
Height: 16 in.
Basin: Brown unglazed oval
21 x 14 x 1-1/4 in.

A five-needle pine and an azalea with pink flowers were planted on this rock in 1972. While there was a marked improvement in design after four years of training, the photographs taken in March and September of 1976 show how much more the shapes were improved within a short period of six months. It will still take a few years of styling to establish the true beauty of this bonsai.

March 1976

September 1976

JAPANESE FIVE-NEEDLE PINE, *Pinus parviflora.*
Style: Slanting.
Height: 18 in. including the rock.
Basin: White glazed rectangular
21-3/4 x 13-1/2 x 1-1/2 in.

In the early spring of 1971 a five year old seedling was planted on this rock. The photograph was taken in the summer of the same year. After five years of training the tree is now beginning to show its character. It may still take another five years to create a fine shape for this bonsai.

197

197

1976

CULTURE OF HEMLOCKS

The care of hemlock, *Tsuga* is similar to the spruce. Canadian hemlock, *T. canadensis* and its varieties and cultivars are readily obtainable at nurseries. They can also be collected in the wild in most of the Northeastern United States. Sargents hemlock or weeping hemlock, *T. canadensis* var. *pendula* is excellent material for creating cascade bonsai because of its natural growing habit.

WEEPING HEMLOCK, *Tsuga canadensis* var. *pendula.*

Size: Height 17 in. including the rock. Width 26 in.

Basin: Brown unglazed outside, white glazed inside, 21 x 14 x 1-1/4 in.

This can-grown nursery stock was planted on a rock in 1967. The unshaped tree is shown in the photograph taken in 1968. The 1971 photograph shows the basic shape completed. In about three years, when more twigs develop, we will have a finished bonsai.

1968

1971

JAPANESE FIVE-NEEDLE PINE, *Pinus parviflora.*
DWARF AZALEA, *Rhododendron kiusianum* cuttings with pink flowers.
DWARF THYME, *Thymus serphyllum* var. *przewalskii* with white flowers.
Size: Height 27 in., width 23 in.
Basin: Bronze oval
30 x 18-1/4 x 1-3/4 in.

The dark red rock used for this planting came from Arizona. It is quite porous and draws water by suction. Planting trees on porous rock is different from planting on harder rock such as granite or limestone. In this case, pieces of No. 20 copper wire, ten inches long, were bent at the center and wrapped several times around the heads of two inch

1976

galvanized nails. About ten of these nails were then wedged into the rock. The roots of the trees were held in place by the wires. The bottom of the rock was found to be too small and unstable to stand upright, therefore, small pieces of the same kind of rock were cemented to the base to give it support. Originally there were eleven five-needle pines in this group, but with the growth of the trees, two were eliminated. A fantastic contrast of color and shape has been achieved with the green needles of the pines, and the dark green foliage and pink flowers of the dwarf azalea. When combined with the white thyme and golden fern, all growing together on the red rock, this rock planting provides great pleasure.

DWARF GARDENIA, *Gardenia radicans.*
Style: Group planting.
Height: 18 in.
Basin: Bronze oval
30 x 18-1/4 x 1-3/4 in.

In 1970 Mary W. Neil brought these dwarf gardenias in one-gallon cans from Florida to the Tarrytown classroom to share with the other students. (Mary Neil has been conducting regular classes at the Denver Botanic Garden since 1974.) These gardenias were planted on a rock by the present owner in 1970 and later shaped and wired as shown in the photograph. The rock was found in upper New York State in 1966 and this was the first material to be planted on it. In order to obtain the maximum blooms, the trees are well fed. They have been carefully pruned and wired each successive year.

1970

1976

SARGENT JUNIPER, *Juniperus chinensis* var. *sargentii.*
Style: Sinuous, eleven trunks.
Size: Height 14 in., length 19 in.
Basin: White glazed rectangular 21-3/4 x 13-1/2 x 1-1/2 in.

In 1967 a five year old juniper cutting which had developed many branches, was planted on a rock in the sinuous style. In rock planting, the sinuous style is preferable to planting a group of individual trees because the upright trunks are connected to the underground trunk. In case of root damage by dehydration in one section, the tree will not be damaged since it will be supplied with water from another section. (This is also true in feeding.) The roots of the parent juniper were planted on the left side of the rock. In the second year, shaping was started by wiring the trunk and branches. In 1976, as the individual trunks and foliage grew greater, the number of trunks were reduced to eleven. It may be necessary to have even fewer trunks in the future.

1976

5. VIEWING STONES

CHRYSANTHEMUM STONE

Length 12 in., width 14 in., height 9-1/4 in. including wooden base. This chrysanthemum stone was found in the ground of Gifu Prefecture, Japan and resembled an ordinary rock. It is most interesting how these rocks are collected. It requires a person of great skill and knowledge to crack the outer shell without damaging the perfect shape and texture of the "flower." One never tires of looking at this multicolored rock of white, pink, and green with its many chrysanthemum flower designs.

DISTANT-MOUNTAIN ROCK

Length 16 in., width 5 in., height 3-1/2 in. including wooden stand. This rock with its deep black color was imported from Japan in 1968. When viewed through the graceful limbs of a bonsai, it reminds one of a distant mountain range.

WATER POOL ROCK..

Length 18 in., width 8 in., height 3-1/2 in. Bronze basin: 30 x 18-1/4 x 1-3/4 in. This pale brown and gray rock was found near Kyoto, Japan and was imported to the United States in 1968. The bronze basin was made by the Japanese artist Houn Harada in 1950. It was especially designed by the author's father Toshij Yoshimura.

HOUSE-SHAPED ROCK

Length 5 in., width 5 in., height 4-1/2 in. This rock was found in Connecticut. It can be enjoyed either alone or with a bonsai. There are many ways to display this rock. It can be placed in a shallow oval container by itself with fine textured moss or ground cover like sedum, or it might be displayed at the base of a Cryptomeria bonsai to give the illusion of a country scene. A carved wooden stand, as shown in the photograph of the Chrysanthemum stone on page 57, would greatly enhance its beauty, especially if it is displayed at the side of a bonsai as an accessory.

ISLAND-SHAPED ROCK

Dark gray on white. Length 17 in., width 7 in., height 7 in. Bronze basin: 30 x 18-3/4 x 1-3/4 in. This rock was originally found in the Ibi River, Gifu Prefecture, Japan and was imported to the United States in 1962. In 1966 dwarf spruces, *Picea glauca* var. *conica* were planted on the rock as shown in the 1966 photograph. In 1974 the spruces were removed because it was felt the beauty of the rock should stand on its own merits.

1966

6. THE GARDEN AND EXHIBITION

The garden shown on page 62 is located on the south side of a house which overlooks miles of Connecticut hills. To reach the bonsai area from the house, one walks through a 20 x 9 ft. attached greenhouse. A corner of the greenhouse is set aside as a working area for potting, shaping and creating bonsai. On a nearby card table, the growing records, photographs and descriptions of over 80 bonsai are recorded on large 32 x 32 inch white cardboards. The bonsai are classified by number. The advantage of this is

Scenes at the exhibition

being able to see at a glance each tree's development year by year.

The house and garden are ideally located on a hill where the bonsai are exposed to full sun all day with excellent air circulation. At times it gets very windy so all the trees are tied to the tables with wire to prevent them from capsizing. When winds are too strong, all the bonsai are brought into a sheltered area for protection.

The tables shown in the photographs are 24 feet nine inches long

Yoshimura School of Bonsai
Box 265 Scarborough Station
Briarcliff Manor, N.Y. 10510

You are cordially invited
to attend a
Special Bonsai Exhibition
Honoring 25 years of instruction by Yuji Yoshimura
exhibiting the
MURIEL R. LEEDS COLLECTION
at
Yoshimura School of Bonsai
514 Scarborough Road, Briarcliff Manor
New York, N. Y. 10510

Saturday
July 17, 1976 — 10 A.M. - 5 P.M.

Sunday
July 18, 1976 — 10 A.M. - 5 P.M.

A commemorative album of the exhibition will be published in the Fall, 1976. For information write to Yoshimura School of Bonsai, P.O. Box 265, Scarborough Station, Briarcliff Manor, New York 10510.

Views of the growing benches.

nd three feet wide in two heights: two eet ten inches in back, and two feet wo inches in front. A one-inch pipe for utomatic watering is located on the our sides of each table with sprinkler eads spaced about every 18 inches.)ne table is devoted solely to rock plantngs. In the spring and autumn, these re watered twice daily at 9:00 AM and :00 PM, but during the summer months hey must be watered three times a day, t 9:00 AM, 12 noon and 4:00 PM. The ther table is used for container-grown onsai. These are watered once a day at 1:00 AM in the spring and autumn and wice a day in the summer at 11:00 AM nd 4:00 PM. Some of the evergreens nd larger trees are kept around the wimming pool and terrace. They are vatered by hose at the same time as the ontainer-grown bonsai on the table.

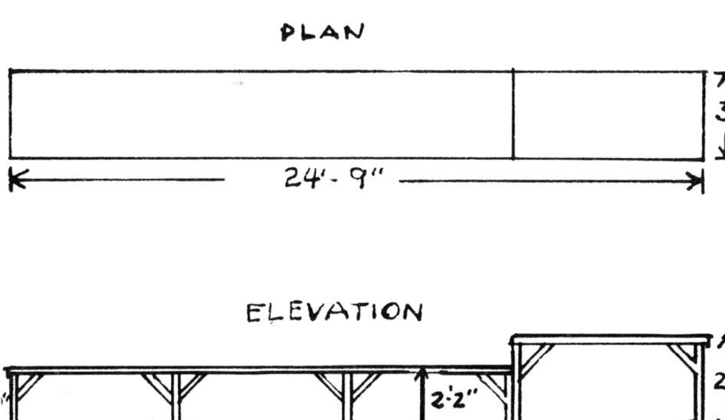

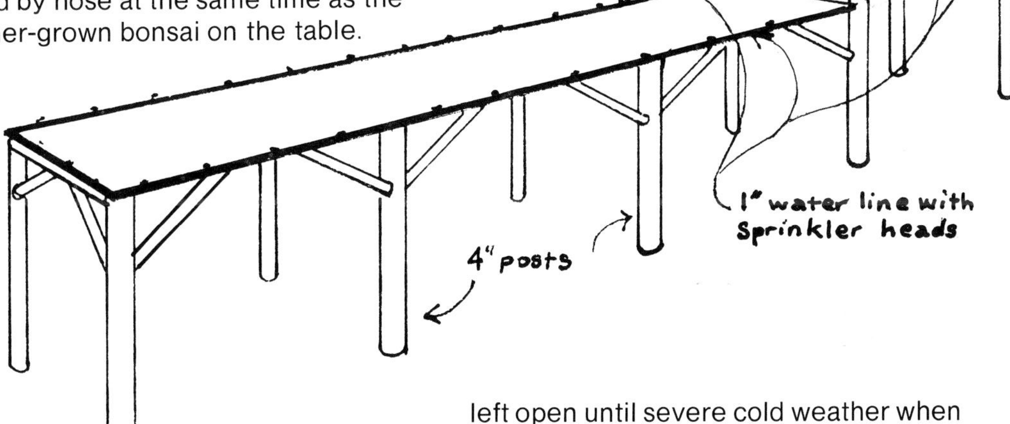

When most of the evergreen and leciduous trees become dormant they re moved to a pit. The clinging-to-aock style and those trees that are not vinter hardy are placed in the greenouse where the temperature is kept t 45° F.

The pit is on the north side of the ouse running north and south. It is 14 eet long and ten feet wide. The depth aries from about seven feet on the side o nine feet in the center. The bottom is overed with one foot of gravel to pronote drainage. The sides are built of cenent blocks with steps at one end. When he bonsai are moved into the pit they re not covered immediately. The pit is left open until severe cold weather when the night temperature regularly drops below freezing. It is then covered with glass, plywood, and finally with a heavy sheet of polyethylene which is held down by cement blocks and wood. Because of the limited air circulation, there is always enough moisture. Before closing the pit, it is necessary to spray Benomil, a fungicide, to prevent the spread of fungi. Once the pit is closed it is kept completely dark. The trees are checked for dryness approximately every two weeks.

Mr. Yoshimura and Mrs. Leeds, also known as "Miss Tiger," as they appeared for the opening of her bonsai exhibition at Mr. Yoshimura's School.

July 1976

BIOGRAPHIES

Yuji Yoshimura has long been recognized for his talent and genius by most serious followers of bonsai. He was "born to bonsai"!

In 1958 when the Brooklyn Botanical Garden was initiating classes in the Art of Bonsai, Yuji Yoshimura was one of the first instructors to be invited from Japan. He had years of teaching experience conducting his own classes in Tokyo dating from 1952. In his enthusiasm to spread the art of bonsai, he traveled to Australia, Hawaii, Hong Kong and the United States.

For ten years, from 1962 through 1972, Mr. Yoshimura taught classes at the New York Botanical Garden assisted by Edna L. Kane. His students subsequently formed the Bonsai Society of Greater New York.

Mr. Yoshimura has been writing books and articles on the art of bonsai in Japanese and in English for many years. In 1957 he wrote THE JAPANESE ART OF MINIATURE TREES AND LANDSCAPES, co-authored by Giovanna M. Halford. This was the first authoritative book on bonsai in English. Today in its 23rd printing, it remains the indispensable guide for the beginner and the advanced bonsai grower alike.

In March 1964 his wife and two daughters came from Japan to join him in Tarrytown, New York where he established the Yoshimura Bonsai Company and conducted classes in bonsai. He continued to travel and teach throughout the United States giving lectures, demonstrations and radio talks. When the Tarrytown nursery was sold for development in 1972, Mr. Yoshimura relocated his nursery in Briarcliff Manor, New York where he continues to teach advanced students at the Yoshimura School of Bonsai. E.M.W.

Muriel Read Leeds was born in Bridgeport, Connecticut. She attended local schools and graduated from Finch Junior College in New York City. The following year she attended Yale School of Fine Arts—first studying sculpture, then painting.

She was President of the Junior League of Bridgeport and also Chairman of Childrens Plays, in which capacity she designed marionettes, costumes and scenery. These plays were given for children throughout Connecticut.

Mrs. Leeds has been a long time member of The Fairfield Garden Club serving as Vice President and Flower Show Chairman and winning the Horticultural Award of the Garden Club of America.

Most of Mrs. Leeds time has been spent as an artist. She attended the Art Students League in New York, studying with Robert Brackman. She is an artist member of the New Haven Paint and Clay Club, The National Arts Club, New York, and The Catharine Lorillard Art Club, New York. Muriel Leeds has exhibited her paintings at various art clubs, galleries and museums in the United States. Her paintings have won many awards and are in public and private collections in New York, New England and Florida.

In 1964, she started studying the art of Bonsai with Yuji Yoshimura at New York Botanical Garden and later at his Tarrytown and Briarcliff Manor schools.

Mrs. Leeds is married to A. Fuller Leeds. They have one daughter, Ellen Read Leeds Sturges. E.C.S

PEQUOT LIBRARY